MEMOIR, HOLOCAUST FICTION, AND TRUTH
BEYOND *THE CUT OUT GIRL*

by
Bart van Es

The Eighth
Martin Miller and Hannah Norbert-Miller
Memorial Lecture

Research Centre for German & Austrian Exile Studies
INSTITUTE OF LANGUAGES, CULTURES AND SOCIETIES
School of Advanced Study, University of London

2024

Published by the
INSTITUTE OF LANGUAGES, CULTURES AND SOCIETIES
School of Advanced Study, University of London
Senate House, Malet Street, London WC1E 7HU

https://www.ilcs.sas.ac.uk

ISBN 978 0 85457 286 1

First published 2024

Cover design based on an image kindly
supplied by Anthony Grenville

CONTENTS

INTRODUCTION

On behalf of the Institute of Languages, Cultures and Societies, I am delighted to welcome you to the eighth Martin Miller and Hannah Norbert-Miller Memorial Lecture.

For the Research Centre for German & Austrian Exile Studies and the Institute of Languages, Cultures and Societies, to which the Research Centre is attached, the Miller Lecture is one of the focal points in our events calendar. It showcases and celebrates the work carried out in Exile Studies and highlights its continued importance, particularly against the backdrop of events in autumn 2023. How could we begin to understand what is happening in the Middle East without knowledge of the history of Jewish persecution?

To welcome Bart van Es as our lecturer is a delight as his book, *The Cut Out Girl*, has done so much to bring the stories of Jewish refugees to thousands of readers. The book shows the value of our discipline in a very poignant way. As the *Times Literary Supplement* put it in a review in 2018: 'It is a reminder of the extraordinary richness of archives and the treasures released by scholarly research'.

In closing, may I say a word of thanks to Daniel Miller for his generosity and continued active sponsorship of the Research Centre. This support is received with enormous gratitude.

Godela Weiss-Sussex
Acting Director, Institute of Languages,
Cultures and Societies

November 2023

*****

We are fortunate to be able to welcome Professor Bart van Es from the University of Oxford to give this Martin Miller and Hannah Norbert-Miller Lecture.

Professor van Es is a man of parts: the last piece by him that I read was a discussion in the *Times Literary Supplement* of two dramatists who were contemporaries of Shakespeare. In this lecture he will be covering very different ground: the Holocaust and some of the literature that it has produced.

The Cut Out Girl is set in the Netherlands and recreates the story of a little Jewish girl who survived the Nazi years in hiding, for part of the time with Bart van Es's family. Works dealing with hidden Jews are common in the Netherlands; so many Jews were hidden there that there is a Dutch word for a hidden person: *onderduiker*. The most famous *onderduiker* in any language is, of course, Anne Frank, who was hidden, wrote her diary and was arrested in Holland. Dutch literature since the War has been rich in literature confronting the topic of hidden Jews and the moral dilemmas and ambiguities to which that gave rise. I will mention only Harry Mulisch's highly successful novel *De Aanslag* (*The Assault, 1982*), which was made into a film four years later. The action of the novel is set in motion by the assassination of a prominent Dutch collaborator with the Nazis – the *aanslag* of the title – and continues with the brutal reprisals conducted by the Germans and their aftermath down the decades. The novel is very skilfully plotted, so I will not divulge its ending, but suffice it to say that hidden Jews play an important role.

In *The Cut Out Girl*, Bart van Es not only aims to present the events involving the hidden girl as history, which must have required a great deal of careful historical research; he also presents an imaginative re-creation of those events from the girl's point of view, a demanding task which gives the work its unmistakable quality as a work of literature. In so doing, he was faced with the problem confronting many of those who chose to write about Jews who were hidden from the Nazis during the War: a lack of readily available documentary source material and the consequent need to rely on assumptions and imaginative reconstruction. It is often not recognized that assumptions have always formed part of the historian's armoury. As the distinguished Oxford philosopher of history R. G. Collingwood put it in *The Idea of History*, referring to what he called 'constructive history':

> I described constructive history as interpolating, between the statements borrowed from our authorities, other statements implied by them. Thus our authorities tell us that on one day Caesar was in Rome and on a later day in Gaul; they tell us nothing about his journey from one place to the other, but we interpolate this with a perfectly good conscience.

> [...] [W]hat is in this way inferred is essentially something imagined. If we look out over the sea and perceive a ship, and five minutes later look again

and perceive it in a different place, we find ourselves obliged to imagine it as having occupied intermediate positions when we were not looking. That is already an example of historical thinking; and it is not otherwise that we find ourselves obliged to imagine Caesar as having travelled from Rome to Gaul when we are told that he was in these different places at these successive times.[1]

But such factually based assumptions only take us so far when it comes to writing history; they cannot be so readily used by the historian when it comes to analysing the motivation of historical agents, their patterns of thinking and their processes of decision-making. The use of assumptions and imaginative reconstruction in such cases risks crossing the line between history and historical fiction. It is this borderland area of literature that Professor van Es examines in this lecture.

Anthony Grenville
Chair, Research Centre for German &
Austrian Exile Studies

November 2023

1   R. G. Collingwood, *The Idea of History* (Oxford: Oxford University Press, 1961; 1st edn 1946), pp. 240–41.

MEMOIR, HOLOCAUST FICTION, AND TRUTH BEYOND *THE CUT OUT GIRL*

It means a great deal to me to have been given the chance to deliver this, the eighth Martin Miller and Hannah Norbert-Miller Memorial Lecture.[1] Sadly, these lectures can rarely have felt more relevant, given the recent horrors perpetrated by Hamas in Israel and the subsequent rise in anti-Semitic attacks, even in this country. You do not look for relevance when you lecture on the Holocaust: it is there at the best of times, and these are not the best of times.

Ten years ago, I could not have imagined that I would ever receive an invitation such as this. However, a meeting on 21 December 2014 radically changed things, paving the way for me to be here today. That day I met Lien de Jong, the Jewish girl who had hidden with my grandparents during the German occupation of the Netherlands. Lien was eighty-one by then, yet, as far as I could remember, this was the first time that I had set eyes on her. I had always known that my father's parents had sheltered Jewish children during the War and that one of them, this girl, had continued to live with them. She was there in the photographs of my parents' wedding. This, however, is not a comfortable story. A row in the 1980s – something about a letter that she had sent to my grandmother – had resulted in all contact being severed. I remember my mother in tears, and, after that, the subject was not to be mentioned. Only late in 2014, when my eldest uncle died, did I begin to ask questions. Was Lien still living? Who was she and what had happened?

My subject today is the place of fiction in relation to the history of the Holocaust. When I first visited Lien – on a bright Sunday morning – I did not think that my background as a Professor of Literature would be especially relevant. If anything, it might be my experience as an archival scholar that could be of use. Supposing that Lien were interested in my writing something about her story, I would need to be sure of the facts. In the end, however, though I did spend a lot of time in the archives, what would take the most effort would not be the gathering of facts but the act of creative writing: dialogue; plotting; metaphors;

---

1   Lecture given on Thursday, 9 November 2023.

5

literary structure. If someone had told me this on that first day in Amsterdam, it would have surprised and perhaps even worried me. After all, how comfortable should we be about the mixing of fact and fiction? Writing anything like a novel on Lien's experiences would have felt presumptuous, even exploitative. I would have said, I think, that when it comes to the Holocaust, we should stay as close as possible to documents and witness statements. Now, having written *The Cut Out Girl*, I have a subtly different opinion: the right kind of fiction, I want to argue, can actually bring us closer to the truth.

I: Memoir

I want to begin, by introducing someone. This is Lien in a photograph I took of her on that first day, nearly nine years ago, when I pressed the buzzer outside a block of flats in Amsterdam and took a lift to the third floor, where she stood waiting for me.

'Let me look at you', she said, and then, after slowly circling me: 'You look more like your mother'.

She led me, with mock formality, along the open-air landing to the glass doors of her apartment, which was clean-lined and beautifully simple, with modern art on the walls. Lien made a coffee and asked me what I was hoping to achieve. I was not sure myself, but told her that I thought that recording her story could be important.

'I don't really have a story', she told me, and then, with no sense of pathos: 'Without families you don't get stories'.

That ended up being the first line of my book.

For about half an hour, Lien gave a me a sort of interview, and then, very quickly, she said: 'Yes, I trust this.' I could ask anything that I wanted, so I started with her earliest memories: her bedroom; her mother; the clothes she wore and the food she liked. That morning coffee, scheduled for an hour, spread into the afternoon and evening as a life came into view. With the light already fading, Lien showed me the letter that she is unfolding in that photograph. It is the most moving document I have ever held in my hands and still makes me cry when I read it, even now when I have read it aloud hundreds of times. It begins as follows:

Lien de Jong, 2014. Photo courtesy of © Bart van Es.

Most Honoured Sir and Madam,

Although you are unknown to me, I imagine you for myself as a man and a woman who will, as a father and mother, care for my only child. She has been taken from me by circumstance. May you, with the best will and wisdom, look after her.

This letter, along with Lien herself, was handed to my grandparents in August 1942 by a member of the Resistance. She was one of over four thousand Dutch children saved from the Nazis in this manner, separated from her mother and father, who were arrested soon afterwards and whom she never saw again.[2]

2   For these numbers, see J. C. H. Blom, R. G. Fuks-Mansfeld and I. Schöffer [eds], *Geschiedenis van de Joden in Nederland* (Amsterdam: Balans, 1995), pp. 315–71 (p. 337).

Lien's story turned out to be much more complicated than I had imagined. Having grown up in The Hague in the far west of the country, she was taken south, by rail, to Dordrecht, where she settled in well with my father's family, able to live out in the open under an assumed identity. Of course, she missed her parents terribly, crying for days on end. A few months in, however, something strange happened.

Lien had been given two little rings by her parents, one gold and one silver. In November 1942, my grandmother told her that it would not be possible for her to write to her father for his birthday. His papers had been lost. When she heard this, Lien took the rings from her fingers and rolled them up and down along the floorboards until, one by one, they slipped through the gaps.

Lien told me: 'I did not think about my parents for a very long time after that.'

As an unconscious strategy for survival, the nine-year-old Lien transferred her love from her birthparents to my grandparents, thus fulfilling the noble wish, expressed in her mother's letter 'that she will think only of you as her mother and father and that, in the moments of sadness that will come to her, you will comfort her as such'. But the horror was not over. In March 1943, a police raid on my grandparents' house, which Lien only narrowly escaped, forced her to flee from this second place of safety.

Chased by the highly efficient Dutch police force, which was staffed by collaborators, Lien hid, altogether, at nine different addresses over the course of the War: sometimes out in the open; sometimes hidden from sight. First, she was passed around houses in Dordrecht, and then, when this became too dangerous, she was brought to the village of IJsselmonde, not far from Rotterdam. Finally, following a second police raid, she ended up in the village of Bennekom, in the far east of the country (oddly, my mother's home village). Only from there, in late 1945, did she return to the van Es family in Dordrecht, by now deeply traumatised, amongst other things by terrible sexual abuse.

How could I tell this story? And how could I connect it to the modern, sprightly, eighty-one-year-old whom I had just met? One problem was that Lien's memory became less and less reliable as she progressed through the war years. For her early childhood, and of her arrival at the van Es family, she still had some sharp flashbulb memories, but, as she was passed from household to household, the pictures grew scarcer and greyer. The last war years were almost a total blank.

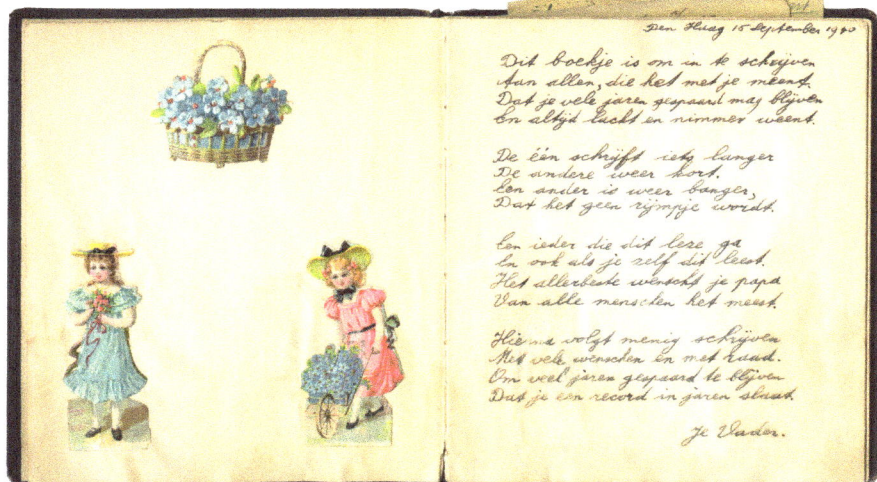

The opening pages of Lien de Jong's poesiëalbum *(friendship book). The dedication by her father is dated 'The Hague 15 September 1940'. Photo courtesy of © Bart van Es.*

Lien still had some photographs, like one of her family on the beach in Scheveningen taken in the 1920s. And she had a few objects: most powerfully a friendship book, known as a *poesiëalbum*, which featured verses and cut-outs from friends and family, first in The Hague and then in Dordrecht. Very largely, however, these images and objects came without very much to weave around them, so Lien was, in a sense, right when she said that she had no story.

My answer, in the first instance, was to travel the Netherlands in search of the places where Lien had hidden. That process proved revelatory, teaching me many things about a country that I thought I had known, and, most amazingly, turning up people who still remembered Lien as a child in hiding, even though she had forgotten them. After that trip, which lasted a month, I found myself in a kind of stupor: I saw the present and past overlapping and felt almost haunted.

On getting home, I began writing and fairly quickly wrote nine chapters. These were part memoir (telling the story of my meeting with Lien and my subsequent travels) and part novelisation (reporting Lien's childhood experiences in the third person). I had planned simply to write the book, but a friend told me that I needed a literary agent. Thanks to him, on 28 September 2015, I got an appointment with a man called David Miller. David liked what he called my 'pages' and thought them deeply moving. Then, over the course of five hours and countless beers (starting at 11.30 in the morning), he gave me some surprising advice. David told me to stop writing and start reading fiction.

II: Holocaust Fiction

There are some obvious ways in which the term 'Holocaust fiction', now a set search term on Amazon, should spark the distrust of serious readers. Simply at the presentational level, there is something homogeneous about these books: barbed wire; the Auschwitz gatehouse; stripes and Jewish stars are used almost as a kind of logo. In some cases, such as Limor Regev's *The Boy from Block 66* (2022), the narratives are based on genuine stories of survival; in others, such as Tom Reppert's *The Light at Midnight* (2020), they are pure historical novels. These are worlds in which the survivors are heroes. At one level, this helps to preserve the memory of the darkest moment in human history. Yet, as with a number of popular history books about Auschwitz, there is also the danger of a kitschy and flattening kind of 'relatability' that makes the survivors active agents in a way they could never have been. Penguin recently sent me a book they are publishing entitled *Lovers in Auschwitz: A True Story*.[3] Such work may or may not be well sourced or well written, but it always pales in comparison to the scale and horror of the Shoah.

The most famous of these books are Heather Morris's *The Tattooist of Auschwitz* (2018) and John Boyne's *The Boy in the Striped Pyjamas* (2010), which have each sold more than ten million copies, their authors going on to write sequels. Morris's book is said, on the cover, to be 'based on the powerful true story of Lale Sokolov'. The author thanks Sokolov for 'trusting me to tell your and Gita's story' and promotional material for the novel stresses its status as a 'document' and a 'meticulous' reconstruction 'based on facts'.[4] The interviewee, however,

---

3   Keren Blankfeld, *Lovers in Auschwitz: A True Story* (London: Penguin, 2024).
4   See Heather Morris, *The Tattooist of Auschwitz* (London: Zaffre, 2018); 'endorsements'; and Wanda Witek-Malicka, 'Fact-Checking *The Tattooist of Auschwitz*', *Memoria: Memory, History, Education*, 14 (2018), 6–17.

died twelve years before the story was published and no transcripts of contact with Morris were ever released.

Whatever its origins, the book presents a bizarrely sexualised version of life in the deathcamp: a world where lovers run between barracks at night; where an SS officer facilitates a love affair between prisoners and takes advice on his own love life from a Jew. In Morris's version of Auschwitz, the Camp Commandant has a Jewish sex slave called Cilka, who, alone amongst the women, is allowed to keep her long 'cascading' dark hair. Cilka 'moves with the grace of a swan' and, when required, sleeps with the Commandant in his 'large four-poster bed'.[5] These unsourced and entirely implausible scenes are expanded on in the sequel, *Cilka's Journey* (2019), despite expressions of outrage from the historical Cecilia Kovachova's surviving relatives.[6]

Boyne's *The Boy in the Striped Pyjamas* (2010) is different. It makes no claims to be factual, is aimed at younger readers, and can be read as a moral fable about the equality of human beings. All the same, three quarters of readers believe the book to be based on a true story, when it is, again, a radically inaccurate portrayal both of Auschwitz and of wartime Germany.[7] In the world of Boyne's story, children (of whom there were very few in Auschwitz) are free to roam the camp and break with ease through a single perimeter fence. The child of an SS Commander is presented as having no notion of anti-Semitism. As with *The Tattooist*, there is a problem here with a novelist wanting to place a modern story, with a 'relatable' modern protagonist, in a pseudo-historical setting.

David Miller did not tell me to read *The Tattooist of Auschwitz* or *The Boy in the Striped Pyjamas*. He told me to read a half-dozen classics of post-War European fiction: Willem Frederik Hermans's *The Darkroom of Damocles* (1958); Fred Uhlman's *Reunion* (1971); Harry Mulisch's *The Assault* (1982); and, above all, the much-celebrated trilogy by W.G. Sebald: *The Emigrants* (1992); *The Rings of Saturn* (1995); and *Austerlitz* (2001). These are very different books from those by Morris

---

5   Morris, *The Tattooist,* p. 271, p. 302.
6   The outrage was widely reported in newspapers. See, for example, Alison Flood, 'Sequel to *The Tattooist of Auschwitz* branded "lurid and titillating" by Survivor's Stepson' (*The Guardian,* 3 October 2019).
7   See Michael Gray, '*The Boy in the Striped Pyjamas*: A Blessing or Curse for Holocaust Education?', *Holocaust Studies,* 20 (2014),109–36.

and Boyne. All the same, in the case of Sebald, there are potential parallels when it comes to the ethics of mixing fiction with the Holocaust.

Sebald, whose books came out in a flurry of late creativity before his early death in a car accident in late 2001, is credited as the pioneer of a new kind of creative non-fiction. His writings, which concentrate on German and Jewish history, blend personal memoir, travel, and biography with photographs and a lyrical prose that speaks of loss and alienation. One central subject is childhood and memory in Holocaust survivors. Unsurprising, therefore, that David should have told me to read him. The first of Sebald's books to achieve worldwide acclaim was *The Emigrants*, which begins as follows:

> At the end of September 1970, shortly before I took up my position in Norwich, I drove out to Hingham with Clara in search of somewhere to live. For some 25 kilometres the road runs amidst fields and hedgerows, beneath spreading oak trees, past a few scattered hamlets, till at length Hingham appears, its asymmetrical gables, church tower and treetops barely rising above the flatland.[8]

This opening description is accompanied by a photograph; together they continue to shadow the author's prose over the coming pages, thus anchoring the narration in fact. The narrator here is clearly Sebald himself, who did take up a position as a Lecturer in German at Norwich in September 1970, and who did drive those twenty-five kilometres to a country village, where he rented an apartment in a grand and beautiful house.

That house, which is described in *The Emigrants*, is a quirky, quintessentially English set-up with servants and a tennis court and an eccentric Englishman at its heart. The Englishman is a passionate botanist, who studied at Cambridge. Only slowly, as the Sebalds get to know him better, does an underlying melancholy come to the surface. Later on, the old man 'confesses' (Sebald uses this word) that he is in fact Jewish, that his parents fled with him from Lithuania, and that he took on his Englishness as a kind of disguise. Underneath this, he is haunted by a strong nostalgia for an irrecoverable past. In conclusion, Sebald tells us:

> The last time we saw him was the day he brought Clara a bunch of white roses with twines of honeysuckle, shortly before we left for a holiday in France.

8   W.G. Sebald, *The Emigrants*, trans. from the original German *Die Ausgewanderten* by Michael Hulse (London: Harvill, 1996), p. 1.

A few weeks after, late that summer, he took his own life with a bullet from his heavy hunting rifle. He had sat on the edge of his bed (we learnt on our return from France) with the gun between his legs [...].[9]

The Emigrants looks and reads like a memoir. In an interview soon after the book's publication, Sebald reported that the story was essentially true, with only the slightest alterations of names and timelines. At first, he had thought Dr Selwyn entirely English, but doubts emerged during the first Christmas party at the great house:

> There was this huge living room and a blazing fire, and one very incongruous lady. Dr Selwyn introduced her as his sister from Tel Aviv. And of course then I knew.[10]

Sebald's rendering of this story of a lost childhood is very powerful and, as I read it, I could not help but see connections to Lien. She, too, had made a serious suicide attempt in the 1970s; she, too, had a stolen childhood; and for her, likewise, I had photographs and documents as well as journeys over a flat land that seemed devoid of that kind of history.

There is, however, a major problem with Sebald's own account of his working methods. He was lying. There was a real person behind the story of Henry Selwyn – a certain Philip Rhoades Buckton, from whom the Sebalds had rented an apartment in a beautiful country house in the 1970s – and almost everything in Sebald's account is accurate, for Buckton was exactly like Selwyn and had killed himself in the same manner. Only, as Carole Angier discovered a few years later, Philip Rhoades Buckton was not, in fact, Jewish, and his suicide had nothing to do with the Holocaust.

It comes as a shock when you realise that Sebald's works are fictions, because nothing in their presentation makes this explicit. Sebald knew Philip Buckton and used a great deal of his former landlord's biography to create his fictional character Dr Henry Selwyn, the Holocaust survivor, and then claimed the story as real. When Buckton's family read *The Emigrants* they were deeply shocked. Moreover, Sebald knew several genuine child Holocaust survivors, whose stories

9   Sebald, *The Emigrants*, pp. 21–22.
10 Carole Angier, *Speak, Silence: In Search of W.G. Sebald* (London: Bloomsbury, 2021), p. 25.

he used, unacknowledged, sometimes lifting whole passages from diaries and deploying them in his fictions, altered but still recognisable.[11] Again, there was outrage from several of these subjects.

Carole Angier's superb biography of Sebald – *Speak, Silence* – reveals that the author constantly played fast and loose with the distinction between fact and fiction: not only in his creative writing but also in his interviews and academic publications. Sebald invented footnotes, doctored photographs, and repeatedly used the lives of real people, making them Jewish when they were not. He peppered these accounts with images of documents such as diaries and postcards, without clear attribution or labelling. Sebald is a far better writer than Heather Morris in *The Tattooist of Auschwitz*, but is his project ethically different? With Morris you know that you are getting a fictional version of a 'true' story. With Sebald everything is hazy, both inside and beyond the books he publishes. For a non-Jewish German to do this (a German who, incidentally, repeatedly attacked the Allied bombing of his country) feels like a dangerous step.

III: Truth

In the light of what I have said about Morris, Boyne, and Sebald, it is tempting to reach for absolutes. Surely, we need some clear lines of division? Fiction should be labelled as fiction. Truth should be anchored in scholarship and concrete evidence. Facts should come with footnotes; photographs must be captioned; there ought to be maps and timelines; documents should never be altered from their original state. In a world where fake news is increasingly prevalent, where conspiracy theories proliferate, where trust in institutions is in abeyance, all forms of 'blurring' between fact and fiction when it comes to the Holocaust feel like luxuries we cannot afford. As a historical scholar and someone deeply invested in archives and verifiable knowledge, I have a lot of sympathy for that line of argument. Truth, however, is somewhat more complicated than the mere accumulation of facts.

When I talked about Lien and her story as a Jewish girl in hiding in the occupied Netherlands, the first name that came up in conversation was, of course, that of Anne Frank. Lien's future husband, Albert, who also survived the occupation,

---

11   See Carole Angier, *Speak, Silence,* on Peter Jordan (p. 268), Peter Jonas (p. 273), Frank Auerbach (p. 288), and others.

actually knew Anne and was present at the birthday party at which she was given her diary. He appears very briefly in it. We are told that he jumped a year at school and that 'he's really clever'.[12] The *Diary* is now the single most important individual Holocaust testimony. It gives the world a vivacious, real person through whom we can understand the Holocaust at an emotional level, and the Anne Frank House in Amsterdam has become a site of pilgrimage as well as an important museum. The *Diary*'s authenticity is beyond question, but things get more complicated when we ask ourselves where the source of that authenticity lies. Most people will read the *Diary* as an artless personal testimony, and I see no problem with that. When we look closer, though, we find that the division between fact and fiction is not so simple. Anne Frank's *Diary* is as much a work of art as a historical document.

Anne Frank received a blank, lined book with a clasp and a cloth cover for her birthday on 12 June 1942 and began to write in it straightaway. On the first page, she glued a photograph of herself along with the words 'gorgeous photograph isn't it!!!!'. She used four exclamation marks for emphasis. Thereafter come the famous words that now begin the standard edition of the *Diary*:

> I hope I shall be able to confide in you completely, as I have never been able to do in anyone before, and I hope that you will be a great support and comfort to me.

What comes next, though – in the cloth booklet – is not like a diary. Instead, we find a checklist of 'the 7 or 12 beautiful features (not mine mind you!)' starting:

1. blue eyes, black hair: (no.)
2. dimples in cheeks (yes.)
3. Dimple in chin (yes.)

and ending with '12. Intelligent (sometimes.)'. This list is dated 28 September, over three months after the first entry. As with Anne's comment about the 'gorgeous photograph', the checklist will be unfamiliar to readers. Both are excluded from the book that we now know as Anne Frank's *Diary*.

The *Diary* – which can seem, and maybe *needs* to seem, like a simple document – is, in fact, a layered creation, in which Anne herself played only the principal

---

12 Anne Frank, *The Collected Works* (London: Bloomsbury, 2019), I: *The Diary of A Young Girl*, p. 11.

part. There were four volumes of the original notebooks, spanning dates from 12 June 1942 to 1 August 1944, as well as a large body of loose-leaf entries. These original volumes are scatty and inconsistent, especially for the first half year or so. Many of the sections are written to characters (such as 'Pop', 'Pien', 'Kit', and 'Loutje') and they look more like drafts of letters to real and imagined people than diary entries. The dating and ordering are erratic and there are numerous lists and inserts such as a very long shopping list for an imaginary journey to Switzerland consisting largely of glamorous items such as make-up, perfume, and immensely expensive dresses. There are a great many photographs on which Anne offers a critical commentary. Volume III of this original sequence was lost. This version of the diary, if it can be called a diary, is known to scholars as 'Version A'.

To complicate matters further, Anne began a second version of the diary, known as 'Version B', early in 1944 after hearing a broadcast on Allied radio, in which it was mentioned that diaries might be of use as a record after the War was over. This second version was intended for publication and re-writes the first. It is much more serious-minded, including clear descriptions of anti-Jewish measures and of the hidden annex. It also gives Anne a more consistent and less flighty persona, fixes the dating, removes sexual and personal details, and makes the whole thing a more conventional diary addressed to 'dear Kitty', quite different to the original books. The entry for 24 June 1942 reads as follows:

> Dear Kitty,
>
> It is boiling hot, we are all positively melting and in this heat I have to go on foot everywhere. Now I can fully appreciate how nice a tram is, but that is a forbidden luxury for Jews. Shanks's pony is good enough for us. I had to visit the dentist in the Jan Luikenstraat in the lunch hour yesterday, it is a long way from our school in the Stadstimmertuinen, I nearly fell asleep in school that afternoon.[13]

Is this fiction? There is no entry for 24 June in the original notebook and Anne, writing nearly two years later is unlikely to have remembered the weather or to have known the exact date of a visit to the dentist. On the other hand, Anne must have gone to the dentist at some point and she would have remembered hot days and being excluded from the tram. 'Version B' comes quite close to

---

13   Frank, *The Collected Works*, IV: *Diary Version B*, p. 643.

being a novel, albeit a novel informed by lived experience with the help of the notes provided in 'Version A'.

The secret annex where Anne was hiding was discovered by the Nazis on 4 August 1944. All eight inhabitants were sent to Auschwitz, where they arrived on 6 September. Anne and her sister Margot were there for a month before being transferred to Bergen-Belsen, where they died of typhus in March 1945. Anne's Father, Otto, was the group's sole survivor and returned from Auschwitz to find that Miep Gies, who had helped them during their time in hiding, had been able to save Anne's papers, which she handed over to him in the summer of 1945. Otto Frank read the diary, in its two versions, in spasms of weeping. When he read of Anne's secret ambition to have her work published, he began to type up the papers and set about trying to achieve her wish.

The book we now know as Anne Frank's *Diary of a Young Girl* is Otto Frank's tribute to his murdered daughter. Otto added no new material, but he did edit very heavily, removing a great deal of material as he blended the two versions to make them into a coherent book.[14] One might call it a work of creative non-fiction. In themselves, neither 'Version A' nor 'Version B' would have been as affecting as the text that Otto created. The Anne of 'Version A' has almost no sense of wider history. Her concern, unsurprisingly, is with friendships and quarrels; sharp character sketches; books; likes and dislikes; her own body; her teenage love affairs. The Anne of 'Version B' – written by Anne at the age of fifteen – is much more determined to document history; she has less time for trivial matters; and her style – unsurprisingly for a fifteen-year-old – is rather heavy-handed and portentous. Otto Frank's version brilliantly fuses these voices: bright and sparky, caught up in the everyday, but also wise and serious and powered by moral outrage.

In a sense, the Anne who narrates *The Diary of a Young Girl* never existed. Or rather, she existed across time and not at any specific moment. She is, I would argue, both a fictional character and a truer version of the Annes we find in 'Version A' and in 'Version B'. Through re-writing, creative invention, cutting, re-ordering, and conflation, Otto Frank and his daughter, together, were able to tell a story that carried a deeper truth than mere facts in themselves could

---

14   Otto Frank's original conflation is known as 'Version C'. This excluded the sexual material in the diary as well as some of Anne's complaints about her mother. Those cuts are restored in the present-day standard edition, known as 'Version D'.

ever convey. These changes are not a secret: you can track them, as I have done, in the *Complete Works* edition. But there is a case for reading immersively, for encountering Anne as a real person in your own imagination, for not thinking too much, in that instance, about the process that brought this Anne into being.

There are many things that make the case of Anne Frank's diary different from that of Sebald. Anne is telling a version of her own story and her father, Otto, has a unique status as her loved, surviving relative. Most editions of the diary also acknowledge the process of conflation, even if readers think little about it. What the process of creating the diary does show, however, is that fact and fiction are not quite opposites. Especially when it comes to childhood survivors, individual, unfiltered witness testimony is bound to fall short of reality, no matter how authentic it is. The triumph of *The Diary of a Young Girl* is, oddly, a triumph rooted in the blurring of fact and fiction.

With this in mind, it is worth returning to Sebald's *The Emigrants* and *Austerlitz*, where the greatest concern is with childhood memory. Milan Kundera wrote that the novel examines 'not reality but existence' and, as Lynn Wolff has argued, being true to 'existence' is central to Sebald's poetics.[15] Sebald talked about the blinding effect of photographs on memory, noting that images can end up replacing a person.[16] He also believed that historical monographs could never be adequate to human experience.

Sebald's answer to the problem of representing the Holocaust was to trust in literature. Through metaphor, fragmentation, temporal and geographic disruption, he confronted his readers with an experience of loss and confusion on an ungraspable scale. The subjects of his books are defined through symbolic objects and structures: Dr Henry Selwyn's oversized house and untameable garden; Paul Bereyter's railway lines; Max Ferber's doctored photographs; and the sprawling fortresses of *Austerlitz*. Our sense of doubt as to whether we were reading history or fiction is part of the effect. Here, for example, is Sebald's account of the moment when Jacques Austerlitz remembers receiving the only picture he has of himself as a boy, the image used on the book's cover:

---

15 Milan Kundera, *The Art of the Novel,* trans. by Linda Asher (London: Faber & Faber, 1988), p. 42, quoted in Lynn L. Wolff, *W. G. Sebald's Hybrid Poetics: Literature as Historiography* (Berlin: De Gruyter, 2014), p. 1.
16 Wolff, *Hybrid Poetics*, p. 136.

> The picture lay before me, said Austerlitz, but I dared not touch it. […] Yet hard as I tried both that evening and later, I could not recollect myself in the part. I did recognize the unusual hairline running at a slant over the forehead, but otherwise all memory was extinguished in me by an overwhelming sense of the long years that had passed. I have studied the photograph many times since, the bare, level field where I am standing, although I cannot think where it was; the blurred, dark area above the horizon, the boy's curly hair, spectrally light around the outline of his head […].[17]

Here are the hallmarks of Sebald's Holocaust writing: the hypnotic, meandering sentences; the spare but detailed prose; the presentation of landscapes and photographs as surfaces that refuse to yield meaning to the onlooker. Everywhere, there is an allusive presence of Auschwitz – the ultimate featureless flatness and place of erasure – in this case, even in the protagonist's name.

Characteristically, Sebald lied about the photograph about which this passage was written. In interviews, he claimed that the boy, while not called Austerlitz, was a genuine survivor of the *Kindertransport*, when, in reality, as James Wood discovered, it was simply a postcard found in a Manchester shop.[18] Sebald revelled in such deceptions. In life, as well as art, he seems always to have had a highly elastic notion of truth. It is possible that this personal oddity made him a better writer, though I cannot say that it made him a better person. His case is more complicated than that of Anne Frank, where all the motivation is obviously pure. We can, though, learn from Sebald's fictions: they are able to take us to a higher and more nuanced truth.

IV: Beyond *The Cut Out Girl*

My agent, David Miller, died tragically early, aged just fifty, a little over a year after I met him, so he never got to read my finished book. I find it moving that his name should echo that of the two Jewish artists after whom this lecture series is named. He had an enormous impact on me, and it feels right to acknowledge his influence on an occasion such as this. When I first met David, I had written nine chapters of Lien's story. That version was called 'The Scrapbook' and it alternated a memoir of my friendship with Lien with a novelisation of her memories. I had

---

17   W.G. Sebald, *Austerlitz*, trans. by Anthea Bell (London: Hamish Hamilton, 2001), p. 259.
18   Angier, *Speak, Silence*, p. 422.

carried out a good deal of archival research and my conviction was that historical truth should come uppermost: Dutch collaboration; the shocking 75% death rate; the documentation that proved Lien's story; dates and sources, including those for her parents' murder in Auschwitz. In the first chapter, I introduced myself very clearly, explaining my credentials and my connection to Lien.

The book I eventually wrote took shape under the influence of fiction (not only Sebald, but also Hermans, Mulisch, and Uhlman). It was shaped by metaphors, first of all that of the cut-out. Like those cut-out girls in crinolines in her *poesiëalbum*, Lien had been scissored and pasted from one place into another and this happened again and again over the course of her life. The repeated displacement affected her memory. Thus, for the early part of the War, Lien still had some vibrant mental pictures, such as that of a small family gathering, organised by her parents in their little flat, which was held on the night before she went away. Lien sat on the laps of all the adults and behaved very badly, and yet she was not told off. That gathering was her own farewell party, but she, as a child, did not know this until afterwards, though she sensed it at some deeper level. The things that Lien remembered were lodged in her mind because she felt loved and connected to people, but, as the War progressed – as she was passed between more and more people – her memories lessened: first, the images of the past become black and white; then long expanses of time become blanks to her. Even afterwards, as an adult, she tells me, she finds it hard to remember dates, names, or places with any precision.

Paradoxically, to be true to Lien's story, I needed to cut out some of the facts and also to disrupt the distinction between the imagined and the historical. In my new version – re-titled *The Cut Out Girl* – I left things hidden. Instead of immediate clarity about who I was, there were descriptions of the Dutch landscape, of the beauty of Lien's apartment, there were metaphors of warmth and colour versus darkness and cold. On the printed page, I wanted the photographs to stand in space without either dates or labels. Although there would be acknowledgements, there was to be no bibliography, no timeline, no family tree, no maps or diagrams, no suggestions for further reading. These absences were important and so was the prose style, which would slip, almost unnoticed, from omniscience to Lien's own occluded vision. Most crucially, there would be whole chapters that conjured up Lien's childhood journey: her witnessing of the Market Garden parachute landings near Arnhem (September 1944); her conversations; the games she played and the clothes she wore; her narrow escapes from the police. Only afterwards would I tell the reader, in a way that might shock them, that Lien remembered nothing of this.

These scenes, one could say, were fictitious, but they were grounded in truth. To write them, I used the eyewitness testimony of others and then placed the Lien that I knew in those situations. I tried to universalise Lien's experience, making her just one cut-out girl among thousands and turning her loss of memory into a metaphor for the national amnesia in the Netherlands about what happened during the War.

I have called this final part of my lecture 'Beyond *The Cut Out Girl*' because, as I said at the opening, meeting Lien changed me, personally, but also professionally. I met her as a Professor of Renaissance Literature. A quiet return to my old form of scholarship now feels impossible. Footnoted academic articles and monographs are an important form of truth, all the more so in a world of internet conspiracy theories. Yet there is also a form of truth in the new kind of writing, pioneered by authors like Sebald, that blends the factual with the creative. My most recent book is a 'non-fiction' novel set in Shakespeare's England and, at Oxford, I am currently part of a team designing a new Masters course in Creative Non-Fiction. A number of recent books by European writers – for example, Antonio Scurati's *M: Son of the Century* on the life of Mussolini – offer what seem to me transformative insights into the mindset that made the Holocaust possible, insights that mere history, however detailed, could not have achieved. This kind of writing is starting to look like the new frontier of literature. The recent awards of the Nobel Prize to writers such as Olga Tokarczuk, Annie Ernaux, and Jon Fosse are an indication of that.[19] Compared to the vast body of historical work on the Second World War, literary writing is always going to be a minority interest: its demands are stringent, for reader and writer alike. Still, I believe that those who truly wish to understand the Holocaust, in as far as this is ever possible, need also to engage with literature. Lien's insight that 'without families you don't get stories' seems to me profoundly important. Stories are unreliable and sometimes wildly implausible, but they are also funny, tragic, human, open, and resonant and, for that reason, they can carry some deeper and richer truths than mere facts.

19   Olga Tokarczuk was awarded the Nobel Prize in Literature in 2018; Annie Ernaux in 2022; and Jon Fosse in 2023.

Further Reading

The Cut Out Girl
A Story of War and Family, Lost and Found

by **Bart van Es**

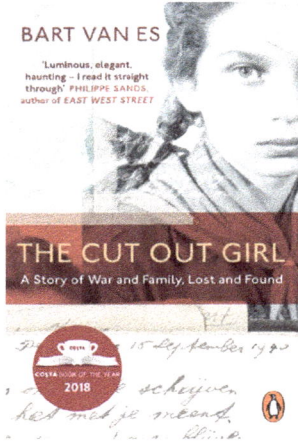

Little Lien wasn't taken from her Jewish parents in The Hague – she was given away in the hope that she might be saved. Hidden and raised by a foster family in the provinces during the Nazi occupation, she survived the War only to find that her real parents had not. Much later, she fell out with her foster family, and Bart van Es – the grandson of Lien's foster parents – knew he needed to find out why. His account of tracing Lien and telling her story is a searing exploration of two lives and two families. It is a story about love and misunderstanding and about the ways that our most painful experiences – so crucial in defining us – can also be redefined.

London: Penguin, 2019 [Pb];
ISBN 978 0 24197 872 6

Winner of the Costa Book of the Year and of
the Slightly Foxed Best First Biography Prize (2018)

Yearbook of the Research Centre for German and Austrian Exile Studies

'… a must-read for anyone interested in the field of Exile Studies in Britain and internationally.' (*Modern Language Review*, 2005)

Volume 22

Music and Exile
From 1933 to the Present Day

eds. **Malcolm Miller** and **Jutta Raab Hansen**

Music and Exile
From 1933 to the Present Day

Edited by
Malcolm Miller and Jutta Raab Hansen

The Yearbook of the Research Centre for German and Austrian Exile Studies   Vol. 22 (2022)

BRILL

How did exiled musicians from Germany and Austria, who reached safety at the Kitchener Camp in Britain, find themselves in an Australian internment camp in New South Wales in 1940? What were the institutions that helped Jewish refugee musicians survive in wartime Shanghai? What happened to Austrian musicians who were trapped in the Netherlands after the German occupation?

These and other questions, and the larger stories they refer to, form the compelling content of this book. Other topics include the struggle of the Vienna operetta composers Granichstaedten and Katscher in the USA, the relationship of émigré composer Berthold Goldschmidt to his native Hamburg and the reception of his 'exile opera' *Beatrice Cenci*. Studies of Mischa Spoliansky's music for the movie *Mr Emmanuel* (1944) and Franz Reizenstein's radio opera *Anna Kraus* form part of the fourteen essays on exile musical history in Britain, Europe, the USA, Australia and the Far East, based on cutting-edge archival research and interviews by leading scholars.

Contributors: Barbara Busch, Hanja Dämon, Rachel Dickson, Albrecht Dümling, Primavera Driessen Gruber, Sophie Fetthauer, Michael Haas, Norbert Meyn, Malcolm Miller, Nils Neubert, Peter Petersen, Jutta Raab Hansen, Florian Scheding, Jörg Thunecke.

Leiden: Brill, 2023
ISBN 978 90 04 54065 1
https://brill.com/display/serial/YGAE?language=en

Publication sponsored by the Martin Miller and Hannah Norbert-Miller Trust

Innocence and Experience Childhood and the Refugees from Nazism in Britain

'With its meticulous documentation, this multifaceted volume brings a range of individual lives and networks to the fore, outlining their inestimable contributions to British culture. It is an inspiring and timely intervention into the fields of exile and childhood studies, demonstrating how inextricably the two are linked.' *(Kiera Vaclavik, Centre of Childhood Cultures, Queen Mary University of London)*

eds. **Charmian Brinson** and **Anna Nyburg**

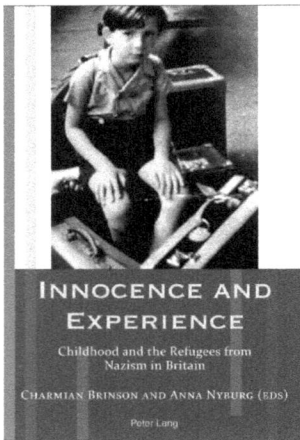

The essays that make up this book cover a diverse range of subjects, all broadly on the theme of child refugees from Nazism in Britain. The book's three sections – on displacement, children in art, and children in education and play – indicate the various topics considered in the study. The authors come from different academic fields – including German and Austrian exile studies, art history, language and literature, and education – so each chapter offers a depth of research as well as adding to the breadth of the overarching theme. Thus far, there has been no study dedicated to examining both the experience of these refugee children and those who worked with them, and yet they and their own children live on, marked in different ways by their experience and making their own mark in British art and literature too.

Contributors: Monica Bohm-Duchen, Charmian Brinson, Rachel Dickson, Anthony Grenville, Elizabeth Lamle, Rolf Laven, Anna Nyburg, Siân Roberts, Ines Schlenker, Michal Shapira, Lucy Stone, Julia Winckler.

Oxford: Peter Lang, 2024
ISBN 978 1 80079 949 3
https://www.peterlang.com/document/1299413

Publication sponsored by the Martin Miller and Hannah Norbert-Miller Trust

Previous Martin Miller and Hannah Norbert-Miller Memorial Lectures

For further information on this series and other Institute publications visit
https://ilcs.sas.ac.uk/publications

The Research Centre for German & Austrian Exile Studies at the ILCS

It was in 1995 that the Research Centre for German & Austrian Exile Studies was established at the then Institute of Germanic Studies, bringing together the London Research Group for German and Austrian Exiles and the Research Centre for Germans and Austrians in Britain at the University of Aberdeen. At the time Hamish Ritchie, Emeritus Professor at the University of Aberdeen and President of the Centre, donated his books on exile to the Institute's Library, forming the mainstay of a growing specialist collection. This has been and continues to be augmented by regular donations of archive material, including the papers of Martin and Hannah Norbert-Miller, and the collection includes a bank of recordings capturing the memories of a very articulate community.

The work of the Centre focuses on the history of German-speaking émigrés who found refuge in this country, on their personal recollections and experiences and on their enrichment of the life of the UK in such varied spheres as the professions, industry and commerce, literature, art and culture, politics, publishing, the media and the world of entertainment and leisure. The Centre's activities include running seminars and conferences on a variety of topics in its field and publishing monographs and collections of essays, as well as the *Yearbook of the Research Centre for German and Austrian Exile Studies* (Leiden: Brill). The Martin Miller and Hannah Norbert-Miller Trust was established in 2009 to support the work of the Centre. It funds bursaries for doctoral study and Visiting Fellowships at the Institute, as well as providing sponsorship for the Centre's triennial conferences and other projects.

The ILCS is the successor to the Institute of Germanic & Romance Studies, established in 2004 with the merger of the Institute of Germanic Studies and the Institute of Romance Studies. The Institute of Romance Studies was founded in 1989, covering French, Italian, Portuguese and Spanish. The Institute of Germanic Studies was founded in 1950, covering the literatures and cultures of the areas in which German and other Germanic languages are spoken.

Naomi Segal
IGRS Director, 2004–2011

February 2011

Martin Miller and Hannah Norbert-Miller

Born in Moravia in 1899, Martin Miller was an actor and cabaret artist in Austria and Czechoslovakia. When he arrived in England in 1939, he spoke little English, and so tended to play the role of 'the foreigner' (sinister conspirators, doctors or the inevitable psychoanalyst). Often these were cameo roles, but they could also be show-stoppers, such as his impersonation of Hitler in *Der Führer spricht*. This party-piece, performed at the *Laterndl* cabaret theatre, happened to be heard by Richard Crossman, the Labour MP, who was at the time Minister for Propaganda, and who invited him to reprise it on 1 April 1940 on the BBC German Service as part of its contribution to the war effort.

A series of stage roles followed: *Arsenic and Old Lace* (playing Dr Einstein), the original production of *The Mousetrap* (playing Mr Paravicini), and Pinter's *The Birthday Party*, to name but a few. During his career he played alongside many of the best-known names of the mid-century, such as Peggy Ashcroft, Dirk Bogarde, Edith Evans, Michael Redgrave and Richard Attenborough, who became a great friend. The list of his film and TV appearances reads like a litany of the British media from the early 1940s to the late 1960s, and included parts in *The Third Man*, *Exodus*, *The Pink Panther*, *Dixon of Dock Green*, *Dr Who* and *The Forsyte Saga*. He died in 1969 in Austria while filming *The Last Valley*.

Hannah Norbert was already well known as an actress in Austria during the 1930s. She had been touring in the provinces towards the end of that decade when it became impossible for a Jewish actor or actress to get parts. After the *Anschluss*, she left Vienna and went to Paris, from where she sought entry to the UK – and succeeded only at the second attempt. Martin Miller, meanwhile, was in Berlin, and arrived direct from there. Both owe their arrival here in 1939 to the support of the Quakers. I believe they met in London and married here in 1942.

As is the case with so many of their contemporaries, Hannah and Martin do not just represent the span of the twentieth century's worst and best moments – the loss of homeland as Hitler exiles, the finding of a new homeland in the UK –, they are also part of its cultural richness, its performance: from theatre and cabaret to film and TV as these grew into prominence (without leaving the other media quite behind). It is to their son, Daniel Miller, himself a major figure in the UK entertainment industry, music producer and the founder of Mute Records, who has worked both here and in Europe (especially Berlin), that we owe the generous donation in his parents' name.

Naomi Segal
February 2011   IGRS Director, 2004–2011

www.ingramcontent.com/pod-product-compliance
Lightning Source LLC
Chambersburg PA
CBHW040825040426
42339CB00017B/485